Teaching Guide

Easy Lessons, Writing Reproducibles & Read-Aloud Profiles to Help You Build Literacy Skills With Very First Biographies

New York • Toronto • London • Auckland • Sydney
Mexico City • New Delhi • Hong Kong • Buenos Aires

Teaching Resources

No part of this publication, with the exception of the designated reproducibles, can be reproduced in whole or in part, or stored in a retrieval system, or transmitted in any form or by any means, electronic, mechanical, photocopying, recording, or otherwise, without written permission of the publisher. For permission, write to Scholastic Inc., 557 Broadway, New York, NY 10012.

Cover and interior design by Maria Lilja / Written by Pamela Chanko
ISBN-13: 978-0-545-17280-6 • ISBN-10: 0-545-17280-2

Copyright © 2009 by Scholastic Inc.

All rights reserved.
Printed in China
2 3 4 5 6 7 8 9 10   15 14 13 12 11
PO # 279110

Contents

Introduction 4

How to Use the Program 5

Teaching the Biographies 6

Using the Read-Alouds and Reproducibles 8

Extension Activities 9

Using the Graphic Organizers 12

Graphic Organizers to Use With Any Book:

Character Quilt, Venn Diagram & Story Sequence Chart 13–15

Connections to the Standards 16

Book-by-Book Read-Alouds and Reproducibles

Susan B. Anthony
Read-Aloud & Reproducible 17–18

Johnny Appleseed
Read-Aloud & Reproducible 19–20

Roberto Clemente
Read-Aloud & Reproducible 21–22

Christopher Columbus
Read-Aloud & Reproducible 23–24

Dian Fossey
Read-Aloud & Reproducible 25–26

Helen Keller
Read-Aloud & Reproducible 27–28

Martin Luther King, Jr.
Read-Aloud & Reproducible 29–30

Abraham Lincoln
Read-Aloud & Reproducible 31–32

Barack Obama
Read-Aloud & Reproducible 33–34

Rosa Parks
Read-Aloud & Reproducible 35–36

Sally Ride
Read-Aloud & Reproducible 37–38

Betsy Ross
Read-Aloud & Reproducible 39–40

Squanto
Read-Aloud & Reproducible 41–42

Harriet Tubman
Read-Aloud & Reproducible 43–44

George Washington
Read-Aloud & Reproducible 45–46

The Wright Brothers
Read-Aloud & Reproducible 47–48

Introduction

As teachers, we want to give our students a well-rounded education. We want them to grow up to be productive, inspired citizens of the world. One way to achieve this goal is to share the stories of those who have paved the way before them; trailblazing men and women whose efforts are still apparent in children's lives every day. It's obvious that teaching history is an invaluable part of students' education—but when is the right time to start? The answer is now.

That's right—it is *never* too early to begin teaching children nonfiction, and neither history nor biography is an exception to this rule. After all, children just love a good story—and some of the most riveting stories in our heritage are true tales about real people! What could be more suspenseful than Harriet Tubman's many dangerous trips by night along the path of the Underground Railroad? What is more inspiring than Barack Obama's ascension to the highest office in our nation? And it can't get much more exciting than Sally Ride boarding the *Challenger*, about to blast off into space! These stories aren't just the ones children "ought" to know—they're the ones children will love to hear, over and over.

That's where the *Very First Biographies* program comes in. We've chosen 16 of the most remarkable people in American history to represent our cultural heritage, and we'll help you introduce them to even the youngest learners at a level they can understand. The emergent-reader text is both engaging and developmentally appropriate, while the read-aloud companion pieces provide more detailed information about each subject. Included in the program, you'll find:

- five full-color copies of each book, allowing for individual, partner, and small-group instruction
- read-aloud sheets with detailed information about each biographical subject, saving you the time of doing research
- a reproducible draw-and-write activity sheet for each title, inviting children to make personal connections with history
- hands-on classroom activities to celebrate children's learning
- and much more!

The *Very First Biographies* program combines all the benefits of emergent literacy materials with all the advantages of a full course of content knowledge. Plus, children will get to meet some pretty special role models along the way. After all, the first step in forming the great leaders of tomorrow lies in making them great *readers* today!

How to Use the Program

You're ready to start using the *Very First Biographies* program in your classroom today—all you need are the books and this all-inclusive teaching guide.

Biographies

To create an attractive display for the biographies, just use the storage box. Remove the lid and place the box on a shelf, table, or countertop at children's eye level. You can display all 16 titles at once on the three tiered shelves. Of course, you may have your own classroom library display system; but whatever the case, these attractive, full-color titles are sure to fit right in. Their size is just right for little hands, and with five copies apiece, you'll have plenty of books to go around. The illustrations are attractive and appealing, and the print size is designed for emergent readers. Most pages have only one or two lines of text, so children can build confidence easily.

Read-Alouds

Included in the guide, you'll find a read-aloud information sheet for every biographical subject featured in the program. The read-alouds are great for providing fun facts and additional background information that children will want to know, yet may not be able to read on their own. However, you'll find that you won't have to alter the text a bit—the information is written in kid-friendly language, so you can read straight from the page!

Reproducibles

Following each read-aloud page, you'll also find an interactive reproducible activity sheet for each biographical subject. These draw-and-write activities are designed to be open-ended, so they will adapt to any level; students can write, dictate, or draw as much as they like. The reproducibles also give children a chance to share their personal response to each subject, making the historical figures come alive. As is true in any content area, when children can relate the subject matter to their own lives, the material is far more likely to stick with them.

Extension Activities

Starting on page 9, you'll find a quick and easy hands-on activity to celebrate the life of each amazing person featured in the program. These activities are not only fun, but also extend children's learning across different curricular areas. For instance, children can use their fine motor skills to make a "powdered wig" like George Washington's; learn basic science concepts as they make a balloon "rocket" to celebrate the accomplishments of Sally Ride; and practice social skills as they learn to solve problems peacefully like Martin Luther King, Jr.

Graphic Organizers

In this guide you will also find three graphic organizers that can be adapted for use with any book in the program: a Character Quilt for exploring a subject's traits, a Venn Diagram for comparing and contrasting two subjects, and a Story Sequence Chart for practice with Beginning, Middle, and End. Again, these organizers are suitable for any skill level, allowing students to use writing, drawing, or a combination of the two to depict their thinking.

Teaching the Biographies

Follow these tips to get the most out of the *Very First Biographies* books in your classroom.

Instructional Settings

With five copies apiece, *Very First Biographies* are perfect for teaching in small groups, or as an addition to your independent reading library. For group settings, use the reading and leveling tips that follow. For independent reading, you can display the books in the attractive storage box, which provides tiered shelving, or place them in a genre-labeled basket or tub. You may also wish to create individual reading packets for students by placing a biography in a self-sealing plastic bag along with other books at their level.

General Reading Tips

Following are some general strategies to keep in mind when sharing the books with children.

✱ BEFORE READING

As with any subject, it's always a good idea to activate children's prior knowledge, which gives them a foundation upon which to build their learning. Even if children have never heard of the person you'll be reading about, there is sure to be some aspect of this person's life that children can relate to. For instance, before reading about Rosa Parks, you might ask children to recall a time when they have been treated unfairly. Then tell them they will be reading a book to find out what one woman did to stand up for herself.

Be sure that you've read the book yourself, as well as the read-aloud sheet, before you share the biography with children. This way, you'll be prepared to set the scene for them before reading. Give them a little background about the time and place.

Use the previewing strategies you would use with any book: preview the cover and title, and take a picture walk. Invite children to make predictions based on the illustrations. You may also encourage them to point out chronology and setting clues, such as clothing and hairstyles.

✱ DURING READING

Take time to discuss any unfamiliar words or specific content vocabulary in the text. If appropriate, encourage children to use context and picture clues for help.

Take pauses to track children's comprehension. You can ask questions directly related to the text (*What did Orville and Wilbur Wright build when they were young?*), as well as more interpretive, open-ended questions (*How do you think the brothers felt when their flying machine did not work? What does it say about them that they kept trying?*).

✱ AFTER READING

Encourage children to ask questions and share their personal reactions. How do they feel about the person and his or her accomplishments? How would they describe the person to somebody else? Does the person have qualities that remind them of anyone else they know?

Give children more information by sharing the read-aloud sheet on the subject. You can also have children complete the reproducible activity sheet (see page 8 for tips). In addition, don't forget to check out the hands-on activity provided (activities begin on page 9).

More after-reading ideas might include writing a letter or postcard to the person or role-playing events from the person's life through dramatic play.

Using the Books at Different Levels

The books in the *Very First Biographies* program are especially designed for grades Pre-K–1. Here are some tips on how to help children get the most out of the books at each developmental level.

✷ PRE-KINDERGARTEN

Show children how to hold their own copies of the books, pointing out that books are read from front to back and from left to right. Encourage them to identify key parts of the book, such as the cover, title, words, and pictures.

As you read aloud to children, show them how you track the print and give them a signal to let them know it is time to turn the page.

As children become more familiar with a title, you might like to try echo reading: read aloud a sentence and have children repeat it after you.

✷ KINDERGARTEN

At this level, children may recognize sight words in the text, such as *to*, *the*, *for*, *are*, *he*, *she*, and so on. During your preview of a book, invite children to point out any words they recognize.

As you read aloud, invite children to track the print and chime in on the words they know. For less familiar words, encourage children to use their emerging decoding skills. Build on their knowledge of sound-symbol relationships to help them "sound it out."

After several readings of a title, try doing a choral reading. Track the print as you read aloud as a group.

✷ FIRST GRADE

By first grade, children may be able to read much of the text themselves. During your preview, pre-teach any sophisticated words in the text (usually content vocabulary). Point out the word, read it aloud, and have children echo it after you. Go over the word's definition, using the word in a few contexts.

Have children read the book softly to themselves as you listen in, helping with decoding words as necessary. You might want to stop children after every couple of pages to ask comprehension questions about what they have read so far.

After several readings of a book, you might invite pairs to do a partner reading or encourage individual children to take turns reading a page of text aloud.

Using the Read-Alouds and Reproducibles

Use these tips to make the most of the read-aloud information sheets and reproducible activity sheets included in the guide.

Using the Read-Alouds

After reading a *Very First Biography* with children, you can share further information on the subject with the read-aloud sheet provided. You'll find the sheets in this guide, beginning on page 17. (Subjects are listed in alphabetical order by last name; see the table of contents on page 3.)

The read-alouds are written in kid-friendly language, so you will most likely be able to read straight from the page. As with the biographies themselves, however, pause periodically to focus on unfamiliar words or content vocabulary, saying the word aloud and having children say it after you. Then discuss the word's definition.

You can also take breaks to check on children's listening comprehension. Can they summarize the information they have heard so far, using their own words? What new things have they learned from the biography about the person that they did not know before?

Keep in mind that you can also use the read-aloud pages to foster home-school connections. Simply copy a class set and send the sheets home with children, along with a short note. Explain to families that their child has been learning about this person's life, and ask them to read aloud the information with their child. You might also suggest a quick activity, for instance, children might draw a picture of the person on an index card and write the facts from the Fact Box beneath it to make a sports-inspired "biography trading card" to bring back to class.

Using the Reproducibles

The reproducible activity sheets provide a great way to extend children's learning through personal response. You will find these sheets following each read-aloud page, beginning on page 18. Copy a class set and provide children with pencils and crayons to complete the activity.

Each sheet focuses on a key event or character trait, and asks children a question that helps them relate the biographical subject to their own life experience and interests. You'll find that each sheet includes space for both drawing and writing, so the activity can be adapted for any skill level. Children can represent their thinking through writing, drawing, dictating, or any combination of these.

You can use the reproducibles for a group guided activity or place them in a center as an option for choice time. Simply place a few copies of the book in the center, and make sure you're on hand to explain the directions, if needed. You can also send the reproducibles home along with the read-aloud sheets (see above) and invite family members to work on them with children.

Once children have completed their sheets, post them on an eye-level bulletin board or wall and use them as a jumping-off point for further discussion. As children relate their own lives to the life of the subject, their understanding of the material will deepen.

Extension Activities

Use these fun, hands-on activities to extend children's experiences with each subject.

Susan B. Anthony There's no better way to celebrate Susan B. Anthony's life than to take a vote! Choose an issue appropriate to your classroom. For instance, you might vote on a book to read at story time, whether to have pretzels or crackers for snack, or even have children choose between two stuffed animals for a class mascot. Create a ballot using symbols or words to show their choices, and have children check a box to show their vote. Collect the ballots in a basket, bag, or box and tally them up, and then post the results!

Johnny Appleseed If it weren't for Johnny Appleseed, we might not have so many wonderful foods made from apples! Try a twist on the traditional apple-variety taste test by having children taste different apple products. You can ask families to bring in donations such as applesauce, apple jelly, apple butter, and apple pie. List the foods across the board, let children taste each one, and have them place a check mark beneath the one they like best. Then analyze the results together.

Roberto Clemente Roberto Clemente was great at baseball, and he was great at helping others. Play a simple game that combines both! Gather in a circle and pass a baseball (or any type of ball) around as you play some music (such as *Take Me Out to the Ball Game*). Stop the music at random intervals. Whoever is holding the ball must name something he or she can do to help someone else! It can be something as big as *feed hungry people* or as small as *clean up a game with a friend*. Play until each child has had a chance to share an idea.

Christopher Columbus Make mini-models of Columbus's ships! Cut out the cups from a clean egg carton and paint each cup brown, both inside and out, for the hull. Cut several large and small sails from white paper, about 1½" squares and ¾" squares. Attach the large sails to toothpicks by placing a line of glue on one sail, rolling the toothpick in the glue, and then sandwiching another sail on top, pressing together to seal. Do the same for the small sails using toothpicks broken in half. You can also create double-sails by placing a small sail on the end of a toothpick and a large sail in the middle. Place a little play-dough in the bottom of each "hull" and insert a few toothpick sails to complete each ship.

Dian Fossey Did you know that like human fingerprints, every gorilla has a unique noseprint? That's how scientists identify them! You can collect children's noseprints by placing a dab of non-toxic, washable fingerpaint on each child's nose and having children press their noses on paper. Another option is to use photos of children, cutting them to show only their noses! (Make sure to write children's initials on the back of their print or photo.) Then pin the noses on a bulletin board and try to guess whose is whose!

Helen Keller Learn a few phrases in ASL, American Sign Language. Teach children how to say "thank you" by touching the tips of the fingers of one hand to the lips, palm flat and facing in, and then moving the hand forward and out, ending with the palm facing up. Practice saying "hello" by holding one hand to the forehead, flat palm facing out, and then moving the hand forward and down (similar to a salute). You can also say "I love you" with one handshape: with the palm facing out, fold down only the middle and ring fingers.

Martin Luther King, Jr. Martin Luther King, Jr. worked to solve problems of unfair treatment in a peaceful way. Help children practice the same skill by engineering an "unfair" experience, for example, hand out stickers only to children who are not wearing sneakers. Then give erasers only to children who *are* wearing sneakers. How do children in each group feel? What is the best way to solve the problem? Lead children to see that physical action, such as trying to take one another's gifts, would only cause more problems. The best thing they can do is speak out and tell you why your method of gift-giving was unfair. To end the experience, make sure that each child receives both gifts.

Abraham Lincoln Make stovepipe hats like Honest Abe's! Provide each of the children with a large paper plate and have them cut out the centers to make a brim. Instruct children to paint the brims black, and let them dry. Then help children staple or tape a cylinder of black construction paper to the inside of the brim, and attach a round circle of black construction paper to the top of the cylinder to complete the hat. For a more secure fit, you can punch a hole in each side of the brim and thread with strings of yarn, tying the two strings beneath children's chins.

Barack Obama Get your class into the "Yes we can!" spirit by participating in some community service. Choose a project appropriate to the needs of your neighborhood. You can have a canned goods drive and donate the proceeds to a homeless shelter; collect pet food or treats and donate to an animal shelter; make cards for children who are in the hospital; visit a senior center and perhaps put on a performance; help the environment by cleaning up a park; or donate gently used toys to children in foster care. It is never too early for children to learn the importance of giving back!

Rosa Parks Thanks to Rosa Parks, the seats on the bus—and everywhere else—are for everybody. Reinforce this idea with a cute craft. Create or obtain a template of a bus in side view, with windows for the driver and passengers. Make a copy for each child and let children color in the bus. Then provide old magazines and have children cut out pictures of people's faces, encouraging them to choose faces of different colors, genders, ages, and so on. Let children glue a face in each window. You can display the buses on a wall and use them to spark a discussion about diversity.

Sally Ride Make a "rocket" right in the classroom! Thread a long piece of string through a drinking straw. Then stretch the string from the floor to the ceiling tightly, tying each end to something stable. If this is not possible, you can also make a horizontal rocket, stretching the string across the room. Move the straw to the bottom end of the string and then blow up a balloon. Pinch the tip to keep it inflated, and use tape to attach it to the side of the straw. When you're ready to launch, let go of the balloon tip and watch your "rocket" shoot up, up, and away!

Betsy Ross Invite children to work together to create a flag that represents their class. Discuss how Betsy Ross used symbols to design a flag for the new country: the 13 stars and stripes stood for the 13 colonies. Invite children to suggest symbols that represent important aspects of the class. For example, handprints might symbolize friendship, jigsaw puzzle pieces might symbolize teamwork, a plastic bandage might symbolize caring, and so on. Sketch the plans on a large sheet of craft paper, then have children paint the flag. When dry, proudly display your flag in the classroom or hallway.

Squanto Squanto helped the Pilgrims plant corn. Children can watch corn sprout in an indoor "cornfield"! You can try the activity with popcorn kernels or with kernels from a dry ear of field corn. Give each child a self-sealing plastic bag. Help children fold a couple of damp paper towels inside the bag, place the kernels on the towels, and seal. Have children write their names on their bags with permanent marker, and place them in a sunny spot. Check the bags each day, and soon you should see sprouts! If the towels dry out, children can spray water on them and then reseal the bag.

Harriet Tubman Teach children about the North Star, which Harriet Tubman used as a guide to help lead slaves to freedom. Show children a constellation map, or any other picture that shows the Little Dipper. The North Star is the star at the end of the "handle." Children can make their own pictures of the Little Dipper by poking holes in black paper, then placing the sheet on top of aluminum foil to let the "starlight" shine through! If they like, they can also use white chalk to connect the "stars" in their constellation pictures.

George Washington Children can make powdered wigs just like George Washington's with a few simple art supplies. Each child will need a paper bag. To create a wig shape, cut an "L" out of the bag. When the "L" is placed upside-down on a child's head, it should create a shape with "bangs" on the forehead and a "tail" down the back (you may need to trim a bit to make adjustments). Provide children with cotton balls and glue, and have them cover the entire surface with cotton balls. For a finishing touch, give each child a string of dark-colored yarn to tie around the ponytail!

The Wright Brothers Create mobiles to honor early aircraft! Give each child a cardboard tube from an empty roll of toilet tissue (or a paper towel tube cut in half). Invite children to paint their tubes white, red, silver, or any other color they think might be good for an airplane. As the tubes dry, help children cut strips from a matching color posterboard for the wings. Simply glue one strip to the top side of the tube and one to the under-side, and you've got a mini biplane! If you'd like to add a tail, just cut a triangle from the posterboard, cut a notch in one end of the tube, and place the triangle in the notch. Children might also glue two criss-crossed cotton swabs to the other end to make a propeller. Attach the completed planes to strings of yarn of different lengths, then tie the opposite ends to a clothes hanger for a fun mobile display.

Using the Graphic Organizers

The graphic organizers on pages 13–15 provide a great way for children to organize their thinking, and are flexible enough to be used with any book and at any skill level. Children are never too young to begin learning how to get their thoughts down on paper; it is a skill that will serve them well throughout their academic lives and beyond. You'll find that each organizer has options for drawing as well as writing—and, of course, dictating is always an option as well. You can even use the organizers for group practice by copying them on transparency film and using them with an overhead projector. Following are tips for using each graphic organizer in the guide.

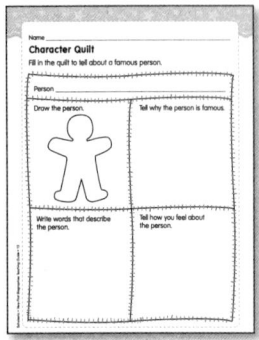

Character Quilt

Invite children to use the Character Quilt on page 13 to show what they learned (and what they think) about any subject featured in the *Very First Biographies* program. First, have children write or dictate that person's name on the line, then decorate the paper-doll to look like him or her. Next have children write, dictate, or draw details in each section to tell about the person's character traits, accomplishments, and children's own reactions to him or her. For example, when telling about Rosa Parks, children might say that she helped African American gain equality and include words such as *brave*, *strong*, and *fair*.

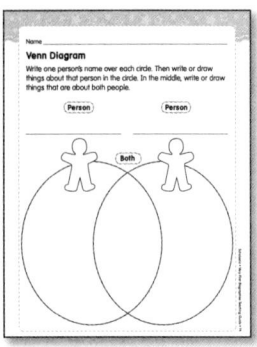

Venn Diagram

Build compare-contrast skills by having children complete the Venn Diagram on page 14. Encourage children to compare two people they have learned about who have something in common; for instance, Abraham Lincoln and George Washington. First, invite children to decorate the figure at the top of each circle and write or dictate each person's name beneath. Then, have them show facts about each person in the corresponding circle, being sure to list facts they have in common in the center. For instance, Lincoln and Washington were both presidents, and we honor them both on Presidents' Day. However, Washington is famous for being our first president, while Abraham Lincoln is famous for helping to end slavery.

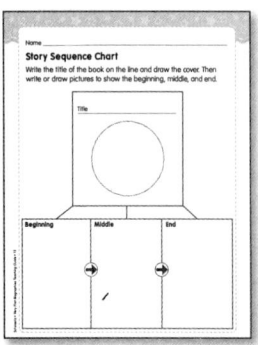

Story Sequence Chart

Use the Story Sequence Chart on page 15 to help children practice sequencing skills. To begin, invite children to decorate the blank *Very First Biography* cover to look like the book they'll be sequencing. Have them write or dictate the title (which is the same as the person's name) on the line. Then have children write, draw, or dictate to tell what happens in the beginning, middle, and end of the book. For example, when telling about Johnny Appleseed, children might say that he planted seeds in the beginning of the story, the trees grew and people picked the apples in the middle, and that everyone thanked him at the end.

Name _____

Character Quilt

Fill in the quilt to tell about a famous person.

Person _Taylor Swift_

Draw the person.

Tell why the person is famous.
She is a singer

Write words that describe the person.
Pretty, creative

Tell how you feel about the person.
Good

Name _____

Venn Diagram

Write one person's name over each circle. Then write or draw things about that person in the circle. In the middle, write or draw things that are about both people.

Name ~~Puppy and friends~~

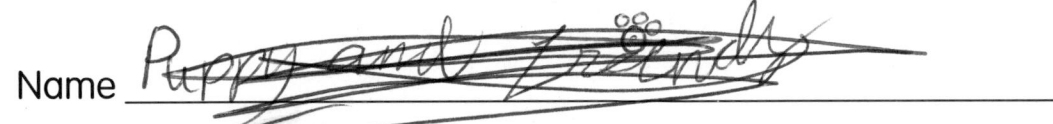

Story Sequence Chart

Write the title of the book on the line and draw the cover. Then write or draw pictures to show the beginning, middle, and end.

Title Puppy and friends

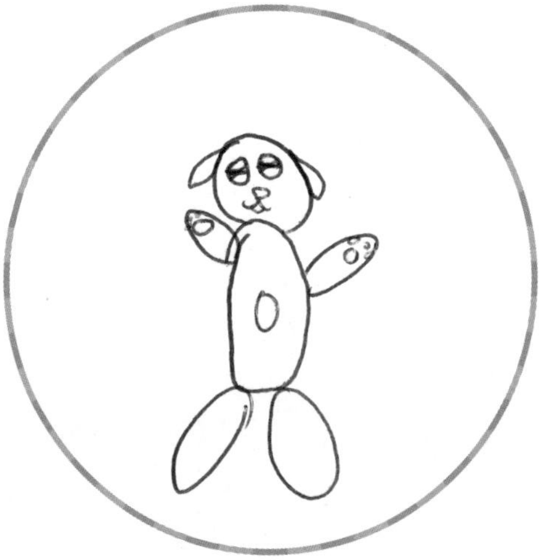

Beginning	Middle	End
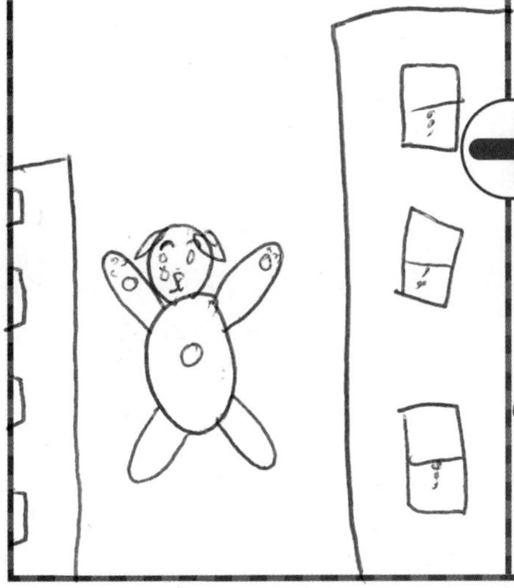	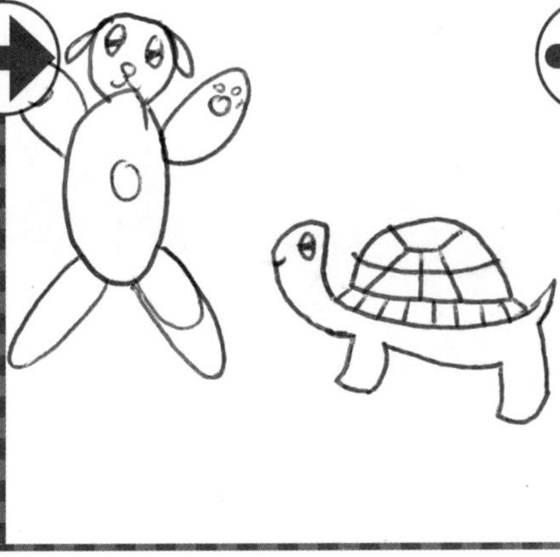	

Connections to the Standards

The books and lessons in this program are designed to support you in meeting the following standards for students in grades Pre-K–1, outlined by Mid-continent Research for Education and Learning (McREL), an organization that collects and synthesizes national and state K–12 curriculum standards.

CIVICS
- Understands ideas about civic life, politics, and government
- Understands how laws protect individuals' rights and the common good, including:
  - Understands rules and the purposes they serve
  - Knows that a good rule or law is fair and solves a problem
- Understands issues regarding personal and political rights
- Understands how certain character traits contribute to good citizenship
- Understands the importance of political leadership and public service

HISTORY
- Understands democratic values and how they have been exemplified, including:
  - Knows revolutionary leaders, such as George Washington
  - Understands how people such as Rosa Parks and Martin Luther King, Jr. have worked to achieve equality, human rights, and the common good
  - Understands values such as fairness, rights, and responsibility for the common good
  - Understands how important figures reacted to their times and why they were significant, such as George Washington, Abraham Lincoln, and Susan B. Anthony
  - Understands the reasons that Americans celebrate national holidays
- Knows the history of American symbols, such as George Washington and the flag
- Knows why important buildings, statues, and monuments, such as the White House and the Lincoln Memorial, are associated with national history

HISTORICAL UNDERSTANDING
- Understands chronological relationships and patterns, including:
  - Knows how to identify the beginning, middle, and end of historical stories

LANGUAGE ARTS
- Uses the general skills and strategies of the writing process, including:
  - Uses drawings to express thoughts, feelings, and ideas
  - Uses forms of writing and other methods to represent ideas, persons, and places
- Uses the general skills and strategies of the reading process, including:
  - Uses visual and verbal cues, including pictures, to comprehend stories
- Uses reading skills and strategies to understand literary texts, including:
  - Knows the sequence of events in a story
  - Knows the difference between fact and fiction
  - Relates stories to personal experiences
- Uses reading skills and strategies to understand informational texts, including:
  - Relates new information to prior knowledge and experience

Source: *Content Knowledge: A Compendium of Standards and Benchmarks for K–12 Education.* 4th edition (Mid-continent Research for Education and Learning, 2004)

Read About SUSAN B. ANTHONY

FACT BOX
Born: February 15, 1820 **Died:** March 13, 1906
Famous for: She fought for equal rights for women.

Susan B. Anthony is remembered for her brave battles to get equal rights for women.

Susan was born in 1820. As a child, she was very smart. She could read and write at age three! But when she started school, her teacher refused to teach her some of the math problems. Why? The teacher believed that girls did not need math skills. After that, Susan's father took her out of the school. He taught her himself at home.

Susan became a teacher when she grew up. She learned that the male teachers were paid four times as much money as she was. That made her very angry. She was ready to fight for change.

Susan met Elizabeth Cady Stanton. They became lifelong friends. They published a paper called *The Revolution*. The paper had stories about important subjects like equal pay for women for equal work. In 1869, Susan and Elizabeth started the National Women's Suffrage Association. Suffrage means the right to vote. Men could vote at this time in American history, but women could not. It was against the law!

In 1872, Susan decided to vote for a U.S. president anyway. She was arrested and given a $100 fine. But Susan refused to pay the fine. People across America heard about Susan's arrest. Many people thought it was very unfair.

Susan traveled around the country speaking about women's rights. She was a great speaker. She became very famous and very powerful. As she grew older, Susan realized that women would not get the right to vote during her lifetime. But she was sure that would change one day. At her last speech, she told the crowd: "Failure is impossible."

Susan died in 1906. In 1920, the U.S. passed a new law that gave women the right to vote. We can thank Susan for this and other changes that have made life more fair for American women.

Name _____

Write About SUSAN B. ANTHONY

Susan B. Anthony was a hero to all American women. Think of a woman who is a hero to you. Then tell about her in pictures and words.

Read About JOHNNY APPLESEED

FACT BOX

Born: September 26, 1774   **Died:** March 18, 1845

Famous for: He planted thousands of apple trees when America was still a young country.

Johnny Appleseed is famous for planting apple trees far and wide when America was still a young country.

He was born in 1774 in Leominster, Massachusetts. At birth, his name was John Chapman. Only later did everybody start calling him by the nickname Johnny Appleseed.

As a young man, Johnny Appleseed headed west. He walked alone carrying a big bag of seeds. Whenever he found a good place, he planted his seeds. The seeds grew into apple trees.

Johnny Appleseed was known for dressing simply and strangely. He usually walked barefoot, even in winter snow. If it got super cold, he'd cover his feet with whatever he could find. He might wear an old boot on one foot and a beat-up shoe on the other foot. For clothes, he wore a sack with holes cut for his arms and legs. He wore a tin pot as a hat. Here's how an old magazine article describes Johnny Appleseed: "…he had long dark hair, a scanty beard that was never shaved, and keen black eyes that sparkled with a peculiar brightness."

Johnny Appleseed was very nice to people. He let them have the trees he planted for free if they didn't have much money. When there was trouble between settlers and Native Americans, Johnny Appleseed would help solve the problems. Both the settlers and Native Americans liked Johnny Appleseed. Everyone knew that he was a very peaceful man.

He was nice to animals, too. He cared about even the smallest creatures. One time, he built a fire and mosquitoes started flying into the flames. He put out the fire and sat in the dark. He didn't even want to harm a mosquito!

For nearly fifty years, Johnny Appleseed walked all over planting trees. He planted thousands of trees in Ohio and Illinois and Indiana. Even today, there are still trees in America that are related to those first trees that Johnny Appleseed planted.

Name _____

Write About JOHNNY APPLESEED

Johnny Appleseed planted apple trees. Imagine you could plant a tree that could grow anything—even things that are not foods! In the box, draw a picture of the tree. On the lines, tell what it grows and why people will like it.

_____

_____

_____

_____

Read About ROBERTO CLEMENTE

FACT BOX

Born: August 18, 1934   **Died:** December 31, 1972

Famous for: He was a great baseball player, but also a great humanitarian and Hispanic American pioneer.

Roberto Clemente was a super-talented baseball player. He is also remembered as a great role model for Hispanic Americans and a great humanitarian. A humanitarian is someone who does good deeds for others.

Roberto grew up in Puerto Rico. His family was poor. To make money, young Roberto did odd jobs like delivering milk in his neighborhood.

His passion was baseball. He was so good that he joined a professional team in Puerto Rico called the Crabbers. Soon American baseball scouts noticed Roberto.

In 1955, Roberto became the right fielder for the Pittsburgh Pirates. He was incredible at hitting a baseball. He was also amazing at catching the ball. Before long, Roberto was a superstar baseball player.

But Roberto felt that it was also important to achieve great things off the baseball field. He devoted lots of time to charity. Charity means helping people who are in need.

Roberto went all over Latin America giving food to poor people. He also held free clinics where young kids learned about baseball. Roberto taught these kids skills and gave them dreams.

Sadly, Roberto died while trying to help people. On December 31, 1972, Roberto rushed to get food and clothing to the people of Nicaragua. A terrible earthquake had just hit the country. Roberto's plane crashed and he was killed.

But Roberto will never be forgotten. In 1973, he became the first Hispanic American elected into baseball's Hall of Fame. He played for 18 seasons with the Pittsburgh Pirates. He had 3,000 hits and 240 home runs. He was named Most Valuable Player in 1966 and he won 12 Gold Glove awards.

Nowadays, becoming a professional baseball player is a dream not only for American kids, but also for kids in many other countries. Roberto proved it was possible!

Name _____

Write About ROBERTO CLEMENTE

Roberto Clemente worked hard to become a star baseball player. What is a sport or activity you would like to become a star at? In the box, draw a picture of yourself doing your activity. On the lines, tell why you like it.

Read About CHRISTOPHER COLUMBUS

FACT BOX

Born: 1451 (exact date unknown)   **Died:** May 20, 1506

Famous for: He was a brave explorer and a talented sailor. Other Europeans followed him and settled in North and South America.

Christopher Columbus was born in Italy in 1451. No one is sure of his exact birthday. At that time, people did not celebrate their birthdays. Columbus dreamed of becoming a sailor when he grew up.

During this time, people in Europe traveled to the Far East to trade for spices, silk, and gold. The Far East is another name for China and India. As a young man, Columbus had an idea for a faster way to travel. He thought it might be possible to find a short cut by sea.

Columbus asked kings and queens all over Europe for help. The rulers of Italy and Portugal said no. Finally, the King and Queen of Spain agreed to help pay for Columbus's voyage. In 1492, Columbus set sail with a fleet of three ships. The ships were called the *Niña*, the *Pinta*, and the *Santa Maria*. Columbus had a crew of about 90 sailors.

After three months, Columbus's crew grew frightened. They were afraid they were going to get lost in the giant Ocean Sea. They were afraid of sea monsters.

On October 12, 1492, one of Columbus's sailors spotted an island. The ships landed on the island. Today, the place the ships landed is called the Bahamas. Columbus called it San Salvador. He called the people that lived on the island Indians. Guess what? Columbus thought he had discovered that short cut and sailed all the way to the Far East.

When Columbus returned to Spain, he became a huge hero. He made three more voyages. He visited places such as Cuba, Jamaica, and Puerto Rico. During all his travels, Columbus believed he was visiting the Far East. Years later, other explorers figured where he had really gone.

Columbus may not have known where in the world he was. Still, he deserves lots of credit. He was very brave to sail across the big ocean. Thanks to Columbus, other people in Europe began to make the same trip. Some of those people settled in a land that was big and beautiful. That land came to be known as America.

Name _____

Write About CHRISTOPHER COLUMBUS

Christopher Columbus sailed the sea and discovered a place that was new to him. If you could sail away, where would you go? In the box, draw a picture of that place. On the lines, tell what makes it special.

Read About DIAN FOSSEY

> **FACT BOX**
>
> **Born:** January 16, 1932   **Died:** December 26, 1985
>
> **Famous for:** She is a conservationist who learned about and protected mountain gorillas in Africa.

Dian Fossey is a famous conservationist. A conservationist is a person who protects nature and animals.

Dian was born in 1932. As a little girl, she loved animals very much. She began riding horses when she was six. Dian dreamed of going to Africa. She wanted to learn about mountain gorillas. She saved up her money so she could go and live in Africa.

Dian lived in a tent. She hiked deep into the jungle looking for gorillas. But the gorillas were very shy. They were afraid of people.

Slowly, Dian gained the gorilla's trust. She got the gorillas to trust her by acting like them. She walked on her knuckles like a gorilla. She made noises like them.

After years of patient work, Dian got the gorillas to be her friends. She was special friends with a gorilla that she named Digit.

Dian learned all about the gorillas. She learned what they ate and how they played. Dian wrote a book about her life among the gorillas.

Magazines and newspapers also wrote stories about Dian. She became a very famous conservationist.

Thanks to Dian's work, people around the world learned about the mountain gorillas. People learned that gorillas are smart animals. People learned that gorillas are kind animals.

Many people sent money to Diane so she could keep doing her conservation work. She fought to stop poachers. Poachers are people who hunt and kill rare animals such as mountain gorillas.

In 1985, Dian was killed. No one is sure who did it. Many people think the poachers killed Dian. Her work continues to this day. There are many people in Africa who follow Dian's example. They protect the mountain gorillas and other rare animals.

Dian is buried in Africa beside Digit and some of her other gorilla friends.

Name _____

Write About DIAN FOSSEY

Dian Fossey went to live with a group of gorillas. If you could live with a group of any kind of animal, what animal would you choose? In the box, draw a picture of yourself with the animals. On the lines, tell what the animal is like.

_____

_____

_____

_____

Read About HELEN KELLER

FACT BOX

Born: June 27, 1880   **Died:** June 1, 1968

Famous for: Even though she was blind and deaf, Helen Keller learned how to read, write, and connect with others. She became a famous speaker and author and an inspiration to people around the world.

Helen Keller was both deaf and blind, yet she managed to lead a full and exciting life. Helen was not deaf or blind when she was born. She was born in 1880 in Tuscumbia, Alabama. When Helen was nineteen months old, she became very sick. She lost both her sight and hearing. After that, she was shut out from the world around her. Young Helen was very frustrated and threw lots of temper tantrums.

Helen's parents decided to find a special teacher for her. They asked Alexander Graham Bell for advice. Bell is famous for inventing the telephone, but he was also deeply concerned about deaf people. Thanks to Bell, a talented young teacher named Annie Sullivan came to live and work with Helen.

At first, Annie had trouble with Helen, too. But then she found a surprising way to teach Helen to read and write. One day, Annie turned on a pump and poured cool water onto Helen's hand. Then Annie used her finger to spell "water" on Helen's palm.

Helen got it! By the end of the day, she had learned 30 more words. Despite being deaf and blind, she quickly learned to read words that were spelled in her hand. She also learned to read in Braille, a special alphabet for blind people that's made up of little raised dots.

Not only did Helen learn to read and write in English, but she also learned French, German, Greek, and Latin! She moved to Boston to study at Radcliffe College. In 1904, she became the first deaf and blind person to graduate from college.

As an adult, Helen continued to live with her teacher, Annie Sullivan. Annie helped Helen. Helen traveled all over making speeches. Her courage and her example helped others to understand what amazing things blind and deaf people can do.

Helen visited countries all over the world. She met fascinating people such as Charlie Chaplin, Mark Twain, and John F. Kennedy. She wrote 12 books including *The Story of My Life*. When Hellen Keller died at age 87, her remains were placed beside those of her beloved teacher, Annie Sullivan.

Name _____

Write About HELEN KELLER

Helen Keller was a special learner with a special teacher. Who is a teacher that is special to you? In the box, draw a picture of yourself with your teacher. On the lines, tell how your teacher has helped you.

Read About MARTIN LUTHER KING, JR.

FACT BOX

Born: January 15, 1929   **Died:** April 4, 1968

Famous for: He used nonviolent protest to make life more fair for African Americans.

Martin Luther King, Jr. is a great leader who worked for equal rights for African Americans. He used what is called nonviolent protest. He worked for big changes in America, but without ever fighting or hurting others.

Martin grew up in Atlanta, Georgia. He loved playing baseball and was also a terrific student. He was so good in school that he skipped two grades! He started college at the age of 15.

After college, Martin became a pastor. A pastor is the leader of a church. He was an important person in Montgomery, Alabama, the town where he lived.

On December 1, 1955, Rosa Parks was arrested for not giving up her bus seat to a white man. Martin led a bus boycott. African Americans in Montgomery and other U.S. cities refused to ride on buses. That caused laws to be changed so that blacks and white bus riders were treated equally.

During the 1960s, Martin led many marches. He led marches asking for such things as equal pay and voting rights for blacks. Martin was arrested 30 times! But he always behaved in a peaceful way and asked the people in the marches to be peaceful, too.

This caused the public to trust and respect Martin. People began to understand that African Americans were being treated unfairly. Laws were passed to help end the unfairness.

In 1963, Martin led his most famous march of all. This was called the March on Washington. More than 250,000 people went to Washington, D.C., America's capital. Martin gave a speech. It is one of the greatest speeches in U.S. history. He said: "I have a dream that my four children will one day live in a nation where they will not be judged by the color of their skin, but by the content of their character."

Then a terrible thing happened. On April 4, 1968, Martin was shot and killed. He was only 39 years old. Martin's work had only just begun.

But Martin lives on, though his example. Today, we remember Martin Luther King, Jr. as a great leader who helped make life better for all Americans.

Name _____

Write About MARTIN LUTHER KING, JR.

Martin Luther King, Jr. had a dream, but not the kind you have when you are asleep. It was a dream to make the world a better place. What dream do you have to make the world better? Tell about it in words and pictures.

Read About ABRAHAM LINCOLN

> **FACT BOX**
> **Born:** February 12, 1809 **Died:** April 15, 1865
> **Famous for:** He was a U.S. president who fought to end slavery in America.

Abraham Lincoln was a U.S. president who helped end slavery in America.

Lincoln was born in 1809. He grew up in a log cabin. As a boy, he went to school for just 18 months. But Lincoln loved to learn. He borrowed books from his neighbors. He taught himself many things.

Lincoln worked many different jobs as a grown up. He ran a store and worked as a lawyer. People trusted Lincoln. They gave him the nickname, "Honest Abe." So Lincoln decided to become a politician. A politician is someone that works for the government. Politicians make laws and try to make life better for people.

Lincoln started as a politician in Illinois, the state where he lived. Lincoln was so good at politics that he was elected to the U.S. Congress. Congress makes laws for all of America.

Lincoln was against slavery. He believed all the slaves should be set free. Lincoln was also very good at giving speeches. He traveled around America speaking about why slavery should end. Soon he was a very famous politician. In 1860, he was elected president of the United States.

He started his new job at a very hard time for America. People in the Southern states such as Tennessee and Virginia had slaves. People in Northern states such as New York and Pennsylvania were against slavery. So the Southern states broke away from the Northern States. The Southern states started a new country.

President Lincoln was willing to fight a war to keep America together. It was a long and horrible war. We now call it the Civil War. The North won the war, and America stayed one country. Slavery ended, just as Lincoln had wanted.

In April of 1865, Lincoln was assassinated. Assassinated is a word used when a politician or other important person is killed by an enemy. Lincoln was the first president to be assassinated. Lincoln's death was very sad. But Lincoln will always be remembered as a great president who fought for freedom for all Americans.

Name _____

Write About ABRAHAM LINCOLN

President Abraham Lincoln helped pass a very important law in our country. A law is a rule that everyone must follow. If you were president, what law or rule would you have everyone follow? Tell about it in words and pictures.

Read About BARACK OBAMA

FACT BOX

Born: August 4, 1961

Famous for: 44th president of the United States; first African American president

Barack Obama is the 44th president of the United States. He is the country's first African American president. Obama was born in Hawaii in 1961. His mother was from Kansas, and his father was from Kenya in Africa. When Obama was a baby, his parents divorced, and his father moved away. At age 10, Obama saw his father for the last time.

Growing up in Hawaii, Obama enjoyed playing basketball. He was known then as "Barry" instead of "Barack." He went to college in Los Angeles for two years and spent two years at Columbia University in New York. During college, he became a very serious student.

After college, Obama moved to Chicago and worked as a community organizer. He set up programs that trained people for jobs and helped kids prepare for college. In 1988, Obama returned to school, studying law at Harvard. He was elected the first black president of the *Harvard Law Review*, a magazine published by students.

After Harvard, Obama went back to Chicago to live. He met and married Michelle Robinson, who is also a lawyer. The couple have two daughters, Malia and Sasha. Obama ran successfully for the Illinois state government in 1997 and served until 2004.

In 2004, Obama became a U.S. Senator, an important job where one helps make laws for the whole country. He became only the fifth African American to serve in the Senate. Obama pushed for laws concerning new energy sources and help for war veterans. When Obama delivered a very exciting speech in 2004, people began to talk about him as a possible president.

In 2008, the Democratic party picked Obama as its choice for president. He traveled all over the U.S. asking people to vote for him. Obama talked about "change we can believe in" and about how Americans need to work together. On November 4, 2008, Obama defeated John McCain, the Republican party's choice for president. On January 20, 2009, Obama was officially sworn in. That means he started his new, exciting, powerful job as president of the United States.

Name _____

Write About BARACK OBAMA

Barack Obama is famous for saying, "Yes, we can!" Think of a job that would be hard to do alone, but would be easier to do with friends. In the box, show you and your friends doing the job. On the lines, tell how working together helps get the job done.

Read About ROSA PARKS

FACT BOX

Born: February 4, 1913

Died: October 24, 2005

Famous for: She refused to give up her seat on a bus. That brave act helped African Americans to fight for equal rights.

Rosa Parks is an important leader in the civil rights movement. Civil rights is another way of saying equality for all people. Rosa fought for African American equality.

Rosa was born in 1913 in Tuskegee, Alabama. She grew up on a farm. Education was very important to Rosa, and she finished high school at a time when very few African Americans graduated.

Rosa worked at many jobs such as helping at a hospital and sewing dresses. She joined the National Association for the Advancement of Colored People, an important group that fights for civil rights. This group is known as the NAACP. Rosa became secretary of the NAACP in Montgomery, Alabama where she lived.

During this time in American history, there was great inequality among people. There were separate drinking fountains for blacks and whites and separate sections on buses for blacks and whites.

On December 1, 1955, Rosa was riding on a bus. The bus driver asked her to give her seat to a white passenger. Rosa said no. She was arrested and fined $14.

After her arrest, African Americans in Montgomery organized a boycott of buses. That means they refused to ride on the buses. The leader of the boycott was a young pastor named Martin Luther King, Jr. The bus boycott lasted for 381 days. African Americans in cities around the country joined in this battle for civil rights; many sympathetic white people became involved as well.

Because of Rosa's unfair arrest and all the attention it stirred up, a lawsuit was filed. On November 13, 1956, the Supreme Court—the highest court in America—ruled that separating blacks and whites on buses is against the law. This led to other laws that helped make life in America more fair for everyone. For the rest of her life, Rosa continued to fight for civil rights.

Name _____

Write About ROSA PARKS

Rosa Parks stuck up for herself when she was treated unfairly. Think about a time when you were treated in a way that you didn't like. What did you say and do? In the box, draw a picture to show what happened. Then tell about it on the lines.

Read About SALLY RIDE

FACT BOX

Born: May 26, 1951

Famous for: She is an astronaut and was the first U.S. woman to travel into outer space.

Sally Ride is the first American woman to travel into outer space. Sally was born in 1951. In school, she was a great student. Math and science were two of her best subjects. She loved reading science fiction books. Stories about space and the future are called science fiction.

Sally was also very good at tennis. She was one of the best at tennis in the whole country. Sally planned to become a tennis player when she grew up.

Then she saw an ad in a newspaper. NASA was looking for astronauts. NASA is short for the National Aeronautics and Space Administration. It is a part of the U.S. government that launches rockets.

Sally answered the newspaper ad. So did more than 8,000 other people. But Sally was extremely talented at math and science. She was one of only 35 of the 8,000 people who were picked to be an astronaut.

On June 18, 1983, Sally blasted off in the Space Shuttle. The Space Shuttle is a type of rocket. Sally was the first American woman to fly into space. She was also the youngest person ever to go into orbit. She was just 32 years old.

Here is what Sally said about her famous flight. "The thing that I'll remember most about the flight is that it was fun."

Sally went to space a second time in 1984. During her space flights, Sally's job was to make sure the rocket engines worked right. She was also the first person to use a robot arm in space. It is very cold in space. One way Sally used the robot arm was to clean ice off the outside of the rocket.

Today, Sally works to get children excited about science and space. She has written books for children. She made it possible for kids to take photos from space by using remote controls to operate cameras on space shuttles and on the International Space Station. The cameras were used to take pictures of the earth from space.

In the future, more people will travel into space. Many of them will have learned about space and being an astronaut from Sally Ride.

Name _____

Write About SALLY RIDE

Sally Ride was the first American woman to go into outer space. Pretend that you could travel to outer space. What would you see and do? Use your imagination! In the box, draw a picture of yourself in space. On the lines, tell about your trip.

_____

_____

_____

Read About BETSY ROSS

FACT BOX

Born: January 1, 1752   **Died:** January 30, 1836
Famous for: She is believed to have sewn the first American flag.

Betsy Ross is the person who is believed to have sewn the first American flag. But no one is sure. This happened a long time ago, and there are no records that prove it 100 percent.

Here is what we do know about Betsy Ross. She was born in 1752. She was the eighth of 17 children! In school, she studied reading and arithmetic. She also learned how to sew and was very good at it.

As a young woman, Betsy went to work as a seamstress. That means she sewed clothing and flags and fabrics used in furniture. Betsy also got married. At church, she and her husband sat right beside George and Martha Washington.

In 1775, the Revolutionary War began. The American colonies fought to break away from British rule. Betsy's husband was killed in the war. Now Betsy was a young widow. She struggled to continue making a living as a seamstress.

Some stories say that in the summer of 1776, some important men including General George Washington paid Betsy a visit. General Washington wanted a flag made. There were 13 American colonies fighting against Britain. Each colony had its own flag. Washington thought it would be better to have one flag for all of America. He knew that Betsy was a skillful seamstress. Betsy had sewn ruffles for some of his shirts, according to stories she told her own children.

Also according to Betsy, Washington wanted a flag with six-pointed stars. Betsy took out a pair of scissors. She cut a perfect five-point star. Washington was very impressed, and Betsy was given the job of making a new American flag.

She created a flag with 13 stripes of red and white. There was one for each colony. The flag also had 13 white stars against a field of blue. America was a new country and now it had a new flag to fly with pride.

Over the years, more states have been added to America. Now, there are 50 states. And there are 50 stars on the flag. Every year on Flag Day, we honor our flag and remember the story of Betsy Ross.

Name _____

Write About BETSY ROSS

They say that George Washington asked Betsy Ross to make the first American flag. Imagine that someone asked you to make the first American flag. What design would you choose? Draw your flag in the box. On the lines, tell about your flag.

Read About SQUANTO

> **FACT BOX**
>
> **Born:** Around 1585   **Died:** 1622
>
> **Famous for:** Squanto showed the pilgrims how to grow corn and other crops. The holiday Thanksgiving is a result of Squanto's actions.

Squanto helped create peace and understanding between Native Americans and the first English settlers.

No one is certain when Squanto was born. Historians think he was born around 1585. He was a member of the Wampanoag tribe. His tribe lived on land that would later become part of the state of Massachusetts.

As a young man, Squanto was captured by English explorers. The plan was to make him into a slave. He was sent by ship to a strange new land. Squanto was very smart. He learned English quickly and grew to understand English people.

This gave Squanto a special skill. He could help connect Native Americans and the English. Squanto returned to his home in 1619. He rejoined his tribe, the Wampanoag.

The tribe's leader sent Squanto to meet with the English settlers in the Massachusetts colony. These settlers were known as pilgrims. The pilgrims' first winter in the new colony was very hard. The weather was bitter cold, many got sick, and there was not enough food. Half of the pilgrims died that first winter.

Squanto told the pilgrims that the Native Americans meant no harm. The Native Americans wanted peace. Squanto taught the pilgrims how to plant corn. He showed the pilgrims how to plant other new vegetables that they did not know about.

He also showed them how to fertilize their crops. To fertilize means to give plants extra food so they grow healthy. Squanto told the pilgrims to put fish in the soil around their crops. This caused the corn and other plants to grow tall.

The next fall, at harvest time, the pilgrims had much more food to eat. They were very thankful to Squanto and invited him and other Native Americans to join in a day of giving thanks. Today, we still celebrate Thanksgiving. The holiday is based on the friendship and understanding between Squanto and the pilgrims.

Name _____

Write About SQUANTO

Squanto is famous for helping the Pilgrims. When is a time that you helped someone else? Draw a picture in the box to show what happened. Then, on the lines, tell about how you helped.

Read About HARRIET TUBMAN

FACT BOX

Born: around 1820 (the exact date is unknown)

Died: March 10, 1913

Famous for: Leading hundreds of slaves to freedom along the Underground Railroad.

Harriet Tubman is famous for leading hundreds of slaves to freedom. She was born a slave. Her parents were also slaves. Being a slave was a very hard and unfair life. Even as a little girl, Harriet was often whipped. When she was a teenager, she was forced to work long hours in the hot fields.

Worst of all, Harriet was hit by a heavy iron weight. The weight was thrown at another slave who was trying to run away. But it hit Harriet in the head. She almost died. For the rest of her life, she would suddenly fall into a deep sleep that could last several minutes.

In 1849, the man who "owned" Harriet died. He had been a cruel man. Harriet was afraid she would be sold to someone who was even crueler. It is hard to believe today, but at that time slaves were owned the way someone owns a house or a hammer.

Harriet decided to run away. She escaped to the city of Philadelphia. Philadelphia is in the northern part of the United States where there were no slaves. Harriet snuck back to Maryland where she had lived before. This was very dangerous. But Harriet wanted to help her mother and father and brothers and sisters escape.

Harriet not only rescued her family, she helped other slaves, too. She led them on the Underground Railroad. The Underground Railroad is the name for the secret paths that slaves used to get to safety.

Harriet made many trips to help slaves. She helped more than 300 slaves get away. She told them to travel at night so it would be harder to get caught. She told them to follow the North Star to freedom.

In 1861, the Civil War began. This was a war in which the Northern American states fought the Southern states to end slavery. Harriet worked as a nurse helping injured Northern soldiers. She was also a spy. She snuck around and learned what the Southern army was planning to do.

The North won the Civil War, and slavery ended. But Harriet kept helping African Americans for the rest of her life.

Name _____

Write About HARRIET TUBMAN

Harriet Tubman was a very brave person who took many dangerous trips. Think about a time in your life when you were brave. Then tell about it in pictures and words.

Read About GEORGE WASHINGTON

FACT BOX
Born: February 22, 1732 **Died:** December 14, 1799
Famous for: He was the first president of the United States.

George Washington grew up on a farm in Virginia. Virginia was the largest of 13 colonies ruled by Britain. As a boy, Washington liked to swim and fish. He was great at math, but not so good at spelling. In school, he had to copy rules from a book on manners. Here is one of the rules: "Do not blow your nose at the table."

Washington got a job when he was just 16 years old. He was so tall that people thought he was an adult. He worked as a surveyor. Surveyors make maps. But Washington dreamed of one day becoming a soldier.

Meanwhile, many people were unhappy with how Britain was ruling Virginia and the other American colonies. In April of 1775, Britain attacked the colonies. America had to fight back. Washington was picked to lead a new army. But the new army was a mess. The soldiers were farmers and blacksmiths who did not have any training.

Washington was a great leader. He trained the soldiers. He talked to them about freedom from British rule. This inspired them to fight. The Revolutionary War was a long fight. The British army finally surrendered in 1781. America was now a new country. It was no longer ruled by Britain.

The new country needed a new leader. Nobody wanted to have a king like Britain. Instead, people wanted a president. Washington was elected and became president in 1789.

It was a hard job. Washington traveled around the county and helped people with their problems. Washington did such a good job that Americans voted for him to be president a second time. Many people even wanted Washington to serve a third term as president. But he said no.

Washington believed two times was enough. That set a standard. American presidents do not hold the job for a long time. They are elected to a four-year term. If they do a good job, they might get elected for another four years. Then, it is time for someone new to do this important job.

Today, we remember George Washington. In his honor, the country's capital is called Washington, D.C. His picture is on the quarter and the dollar bill. All over the country, there are streets, bridges, and mountains named after Washington.

Name _____

Write About GEORGE WASHINGTON

Because George Washington was the first leader of our country, the capital is named after him. Think of a place that you would like to be the leader of, and have named after you! In the box, draw a picture of your place. On the lines, tell why you chose it.

Read About THE WRIGHT BROTHERS

> **FACT BOX**
> **Born:** Wilbur (April 16, 1867); Orville (August 19, 1871)
> **Died:** Wilbur (May 30, 1912); Orville (January 30, 1948)
> **Famous for:** They followed their dreams and invented the airplane.

The Wright brothers were super-talented inventors. They built the very first airplane. Wilbur was the big brother. He was four years older than Orville. When they were little kids, their father bought them a flying toy. They played with it so much that they soon broke it.

Forever after, the Wright Brothers were fascinated by the idea of flight. Wilbur read books to learn how birds fly. Orville made kites and sold them at school. The Wright Brothers were good students, but they did not finish high school. That was not unusual in those days. The brothers went into business together. First they opened a printing shop and later they opened a bicycle shop.

The brothers continued to dream of flying, so they decided to build a flying machine. It would have an engine and controls.

Before trying their machine, the brothers learned all about air and wind. They read books and did experiments. They tested small models of their flying machine. The Wright brothers were very careful. When they were pretty certain it would work, they built a full-size flying machine.

They decided to try out their invention at Kitty Hawk in North Carolina. Kitty Hawk is near the ocean. All the sand and water could be a cushion if their flying machine crashed.

The brothers flipped a coin to see who would get the first try. Wilbur went first. But the flying machine's engine sputtered and quickly stopped. The machine crashed before it could take off. The brothers spent several days fixing their invention.

On December 17, 1903, they tried to fly again. This time it was Orville's turn. The machine lifted off and traveled 120 feet. It was up in the air for 12 seconds. The Wright brothers had done it! They had invented a flying machine!

The Wright brother's invention became known as an airplane. The brothers built better planes. The new planes flew longer and higher. They started an airplane company.

If you happen to ride in an airplane, think of the Wright brothers. This is their invention. They did it first.

Name _____

Write About THE WRIGHT BROTHERS

The Wright brothers had to keep on trying until they could get their airplane to fly. Think of something that you had to try very hard to learn how to do. Then tell about it in pictures and words.